The Illustrated Declaration of Arbroath

SALTIRE
SOCIETY
SCOTLAND

COMANN
CRANN
NA H-ALBA

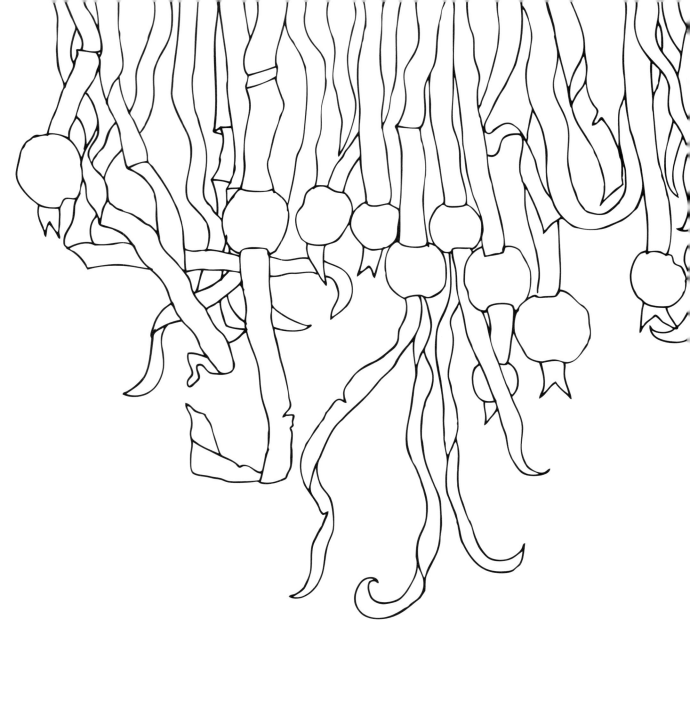

Published by the Saltire Society 2019
9 Fountain Close
22 High Street
Edinburgh EH1 1TF
SC 04962

Copyright © Andrew Redmond Barr 2019
Foreword copyright © Alan Riach 2019
Printed and bound by Bell & Bain, Scotland

A catalogue record for this book is available from the
British Library.

ISBN 9780854111244

Author portraits by Josh Bircham of Pict Digital

To rebels everywhere

TABLE OF CONTENTS

FOREWORD

Alan Riach, Professor of Scottish Literature

The Declaration of Arbroath belongs to a particular time and place, but equally, its power as a political statement has lasting mythical status, about which we are wise to be careful, but from which we also might draw strength.

It is, for me, not only a document from history but a work of literature, words organised by laws of both self-conscious rhetoric and emotional intuition, lastingly memorable, which commands respect and imaginative engagement.

The literary sophistication at work in the Declaration is an extraordinary example of what writing can do. Lord Cooper, judge and historian, described it as a 'remarkable manifesto': 'Read it again, and judge for yourselves whether it does not deserve on its merits to be ranked as one of the masterpieces of political rhetoric of all time.'

Andrew Redmond Barr, in this account, draws a fine line threading between the material of history, the engagement of his own personal story, including his own family background, and the affirmation of political allegiance, which means that this book is his own and yet feels both commemorative and of immediate significance. In this regard it is a natural successor to his first book, *Summer of Independence: Stories from a Nation in the Making.* It is the work of a keen aesthetic intelligence, characterised by humane sympathy and outward-looking national commitment. It is an investment in matters of value, like the original Declaration itself.

Andrew is someone knows how, and where, to draw that line, to make connections, to make distinctions between things, to safeguard what we value and keep what would oppose such value out. And to pull on that line what is of greatest worth from a personal, political, and national standpoint, from the distant past all the way up into the present, is what makes this book so unique, and so worthwhile.

Sanctissimo Patri in Christo ac Domino, domino Johanni, divina providencia Sacrosancte Romane et Universalis Ecclesie Summo Pontifici, Filii Sui Humiles et devoti Duncanus Comes de Fyf, Thomas Ranulphi Comes Moravie Dominus Manniæ et Vallis Anandie, Patricius de Dunbar Comes Marchie Malisius Comes de Stratherne, Malcolmus Comes de Leuenax, Willelmus Comes de Roos, Magnus Comes Cathanie Et Orkadie Et Willelmus Comes Suthirlandie; Walterus Senescallus Scocie Willelmus de Soules Buttonarius Scocie, Jacobus Dominus de Duglas, Rogerus de Moubray, David de Graham, Ingeramus de Umphraville, Johannes de Menetethe Custos Comitatus de Menetethe, Alexander de Abernethy, Gilbertus de Haya Constabularius Scocie, Robertus de Keth Marscallus Scocie, Henricus de Sancto claro, Johannes de Graham, David de Lindesay, Willelmus Oliphant, Patricius de Graham, Johannes de Fentoun, Willelmus de Abirnethy, David de Wemys, Willelmus de Ramesay, Willelmus de Monte alto, Fergusius de Ardrossan, Eustacius de Maxwell, Willelmus de Ramesay, Willelmus de Mushet, Fergusius de Ardrossan, et ceteri Barones et Libere tenentes ac tota Communitas Regni Scocie, omnimodam Reverenciam filialem cum devotis pedum osculis beatorum. Quorum Scimus, Sanctissime Pater et Domine, et ex antiquorum gestis et Libris Collegimus quod inter ceteras nacones egregias nostra scilicet Scottorum nacio multis fuerit preconiis predicata, que de Maiori Scithia per Mare tirenum et Columpnas Herculis transiens et in hispania inter ferocissimas gentes per multa temporum curricula residens a nullis quantumcumque barbaricis poterat allicubi gentibus subiugari. Indeque veniens post mille et ducentos annos a transitu populi israelitici per mare rubrum sibi sedes in occidente quas nunc optinet, expulsis primo Britonibus et Anglicis saepius, multis cum victoriis et Laboribus quamplurimis adquisivit, easque ab omni servitute liberas ut priscorum testatur Historia semper tenuit et reguum Regni Centum et Tredecim Reges de ipsorum Regali prosapia, nullo alienigena interveniente, cuReganavit. Quorum Nobilitatem et Merita, licet ex aliis non clarerent, satis patenter effulgent ex eo quod Rex Regum et dominancium dominus Ihesus Christus post passionem suam fidem Sacratissimam convocavit Nec eos per quemlibet in dicta fide confirmari voluit set suum primum apostolum licet ordine secundum vel tercium Sanctum Andream, mitissimum beati Petri Germanum quem ipsos preesse voluit et patronum. He autem Sanctissimi Patres et Predecessores vestri sollicita mente pensantes ipsum Regnum et populum ut beati Petri germani peculium multis favoribus et privilegiis quamplurimis munierunt, Ita quippe quod gens nostra sub ipsorum protectione hucusque libera degit et quieta donec ille princeps Magnificus Rex Anglorum Edwardus, pater istius qui nunc est, Regnum nostrum acephalum populumque nullius mali aut doli conscium nec bellis aut consuetis tunc assuetum sub amici et confederati specie inimicabiliter infestavit. Cuius in iuras Ceterat

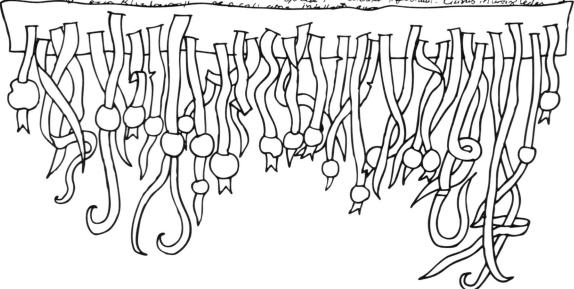

PROLOGUE

Ever since I first read about the Declaration of Arbroath it has lived in my imagination as an icon of Scottish independence. Its image is recognised throughout Scotland, and far beyond, because as well as being known for the message it contains it is also visually distinctive; a parchment letter with a thick morass of wax seals on ribbons hanging below, the signatures of Scots magnates and nobles tied one over the other, clustered and tangled as if attached in popular flurry. You can almost imagine the weight of it, and the unexpected delight of its creators in finding so many so eager to sign.

The Declaration of Arbroath was a diplomatic letter sent from the Scots to the Pope in 1320, calling for Scotland to be recognised as an independent kingdom against English claims of overlordship. Though written in the bleakest times of war and violence, this Declaration spoke to the most basic human desires for freedom and peace, and revealed something profound about Scotland's earliest ideas of people-power, liberty

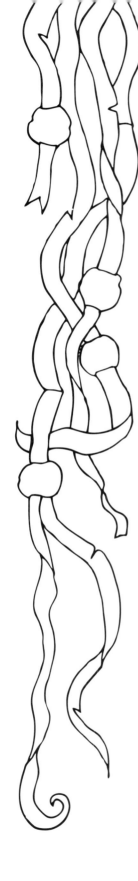

and nationhood. It represented an idea of Scotland so often almost lost and defeated throughout the ages, but always somehow mended and restored.

It is in the spirit of remaking that I approach the Declaration of Arbroath on its 700th anniversary. The Declaration lends itself naturally to illustration because the text itself is rich in images. Its message conjures a picture of a nation somewhat embattled and under siege, but also a nation hopeful for transformation, a nation ripe with stories and traditions and a nation in touch with Europe and its place in the wider world.

There has been a great volume of academic research into the Declaration of Arbroath and the Wars of Scottish Independence, much of which has been invaluable in the making of this book. I am not an academic but a writer and artist with a view that our history needs room to breathe outwith academia, and that artistic interpretation can aid our understanding of the past.

The life of a nation, like the life of a person, is a complex puzzle of episodes and events from which we try to find the threads of a story. What our most ancient texts lack in verifiable accuracy they make up for in another kind of truth, a bardic truth, a sense of how the country once felt, what people believed in, what frightened them and what gave them hope. All of this can be lost when history is reduced to dates, times, numbers and names. The chroniclers of the old Scotland were tale-tellers, and their tale-telling revealed something truthful about the time and place in which they lived.

First, it should be understood that the wars of conquest waged against Scotland in the Middle Ages were not simply designed to defeat the Scots army in battle, but to erase the very idea of Scotland from memory. All Scottish thought, Scottish art and Scottish writing today exists because an idea of Scotland, against all the odds, survived.

The Declaration of Arbroath remains today one of Scotland's most cherished historical treasures. Its value is not in the parchment artefact itself but in the resonance of the words, the defiance of tyranny, the power of the people, the survival of Scotland – those words, 'for freedom alone', which still linger and lurk in the deep memory of the nation. Its image remains a permanent reminder of those Scottish rights so often lost and re-won throughout history, and the rights which in the eyes of many are yet to be won for a final time.

The written word has a long and enduring place in Scottish political life, and the Declaration of Arbroath rings sharply through the ages as perhaps our greatest ever demonstration of word-power. Today there are many people around the world seeking freedoms of different kinds, and my hope is that the Declaration of Arbroath on its 700th anniversary will reaffirm a sense that the written word and the freedom to write are vital to human expression and ought to be defended.

Centuries after it was first written, the Declaration of Arbroath still has something relevant to say about the world. The principle of the sovereignty of the people in particular endures through the ages. The assertion

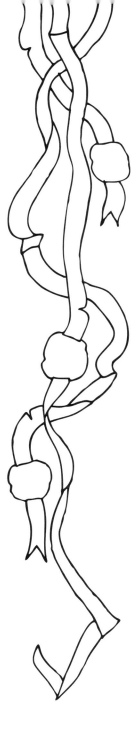

of the people's demands over and above that of kings, parliaments, governments or political leaders, is today just as powerful an idea, and just as hotly contested.

The Declaration of Arbroath therefore is not only one of the primary foundation stones of Scottish identity, it is also the original document of Scottish democratic thought, a thread of which has found its way through centuries of cultural and political change to this very moment.

To me the Declaration of Arbroath is a manifestation, a solidification, an illustration, of all that is fascinating, curious and uplifting about this country I wasn't born in, but which I call my home. 700 years since the Declaration of Arbroath was written, Scotland stands yet again in a state of flux, toying once more with new ideas of nationhood and independence.

In creating this book I hope, in my small part, to celebrate Scotland's historic presence in the world community, and to contribute as best I can to the carrying stream of this ancient but ever-evolving country. Illuminate our history and our history will illuminate us in return; that is the principal at the core of this book.

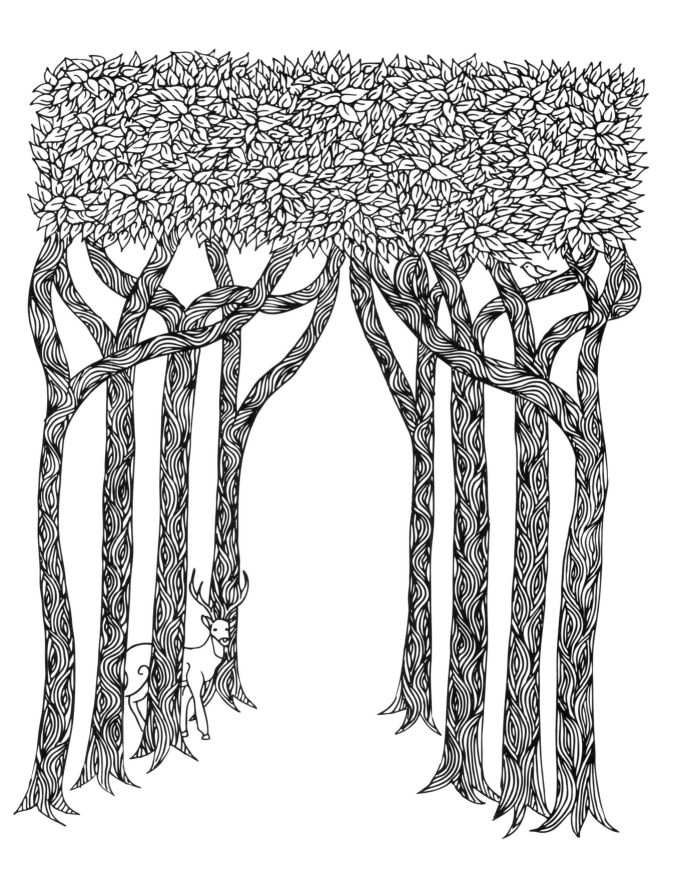

A Sair Fecht

By the time a Kingdom of Scotland was founded its history was already long. People had for centuries made their mark across the country in settlements, clearings, farmland and forts. Their simple technologies and guerrilla warfare had by some miracle staved off the invading armies of the mighty Roman Empire. These early people were hardy and independent, and according to Roman records were led by a bard-like firebrand named Calgacus to defend their native country. They did not yet recognise themselves as Scots, but their memory would set the premise for Scots to come.

Over time a long line of Pictish rulers gave way to an all-encompassing Pictish-Gaelic Scottish Kingdom, *Rìoghachd na h-Alba*. This mountainous realm stretched across the fields and forests of the country from the Atlantic to the North Sea, and a long line of kings kept the land free and independent for hundreds of years. It established monasteries and abbeys, built market towns, minted the first Scottish currencies, and traded with neighbours in both England and Europe.

The first sign of trouble came in 1286, with the unexpected death of King Alexander III. The king had vanished one night during a storm as he made his way along the clifftops near Kinghorn in Fife. The following morning, as the skies cleared and the sun rose, his body was found face-down in the sand. The Scottish king was dead, leaving no immediate heir to the crown.

The death of Alexander III was Scotland's first taste of the instability and constitutional turmoil which would threaten the very survival of the kingdom. The king's tragic fall marked a profound turning-point, one of the great what-ifs of Scottish history, which set in motion a sequence of events that changed the fate of the nation and would lead, many years later, to the writing of the Declaration of Arbroath.

A vacuum was thrown open in which Scotland would soon not only have to summon leadership from bitter internal rivals, but fight for its very existence as a nation.

Before long a rumble was heard from Scotland's powerful southern neighbour. Without an heir to its crown the Scottish kingdom was vulnerable, and soon Edward I of England maneuvered himself to stake a claim over Scotland. Edward's claim of overlordship was baseless, but it was backed by a powerful English army. A relative of mine, the Rev. James Barr, put it bluntly when he said Edward's claim was 'the most flimsy and ludicrous ever hurled at a free people.'

The English position might have been flimsy, but the Scots had no leader to defend them from invasion, nor did they have much in the way of an army except

for the early makings of a small *Servitium Scotticanum*, a Scottish Service, which was no real match for the professional English force.

King Edward's first ambition was to appoint a puppet ruler to govern Scotland on his behalf, but he soon found his appetite for conquest unfulfilled. His mind turned to complete occupation, and he sent an army northward to take possession of the towns and the land. Edward sought not only the military defeat of Scottish defences but something far more profound: the very abolition Scotland as an idea. Anything which reminded the Scots of their distinct nationality, from books, treaties and records, to monuments, relics and artefacts, was to be stolen, burnt or destroyed.

From the abbey at Scone the English army removed the Stone of Destiny, the ancient crowning-stone of Scottish kings, and carried it south to London. The Stone was then embedded beneath the English Coronation Chair so that, in theory, whoever was crowned King of England would be Overlord of Scotland as well. The symbolism was a deliberate humiliation. Scotland was to be contained, sat upon, snuffed out.

Further humiliation came when a raft of Scottish nobles, seeing little chance of survival, pledged themselves to Edward and fled south to enjoy the rewards of fertile English estates. But the Scots of the villages and towns were still adamant they were Scots, with or without a king, with or without their books, their records, their relics, their Stone.

Something extraordinary began to develop in the Scottish psyche. An idea of Scotland survived beyond its physical artefacts and towns. The inklings of a powerful idea began to take hold; that a nation did not exist because it had a king, nor because it had regalia of state, but because it believed in itself as a community. A nation did not belong to kings, nobles or claimants to the throne, but to some other body, a body of the populace, a community of the realm. All the more profound this idea became as its first champions, William Wallace and Andrew de Moray, emerged to rouse people from the villages and towns to fight for their country's survival.

According to the poet Blind Harry, William Wallace was called to fight in a dream in which he saw all of Scotland on fire from Ross to the Solway Firth. An old man, St Andrew, presented him with a sword with which to free his people, and when Wallace awoke from this vision he knew what had to be done.

Wallace empowered the Scots. No more were they at the sole command of those born to rule. Now the Scots as a people, as a community, asserted themselves, made themselves guardians of their own country, and went to war of their own volition. A bond was made between people and nation the likes of which was practically unknown elsewhere in Europe at the time.

Wallace's uprisings were fervent but carefully targeted, deploying guerrilla tactics to burn out the English garrisons. But they also came with a heavy toll. The Scots were heavily outnumbered, poorly equipped, poorly trained and kingless. Their primary towns were burnt out, their only neighbour was a tyrant, conquest was always imminent, and the odds were stacked

against them. In Blind Harry's accounts there was a bardic quality to Wallace; his brilliant oratories gave his followers, despite everything, a miraculous hope for deliverance.

But not all Scots were enamoured with this new popular hero. Jealous Scottish nobles were suspicious to see a man of lower rank build such a loyal and dedicated following. The chronicler Walter Bower angrily rebuked these nobles in his writing: 'Why is covetous envy so much in control in Scotland? How sad that it is natural for Scots to detest not only the happiness of other people, but also the happiness of their own countrymen.'

Nonetheless, Wallace and de Moray carried on through the villages, with or without noble support, and common people thronged to them. They waged a summer campaign culminating in a remarkable victory at the Battle of Stirling Bridge. The victors urgently despatched letters to the German cities of Lübeck and Hamburg, stating that Scotland was once again a free and independent nation seeking to reopen trade with Europe.

But Edward wasn't finished. His armies struck heavily, again and again, sacking and burning Scottish towns and annexing the country with garrisons. The Scots were exhausted, but they were encouraged by the words of their best orators and the dream of a free country. They took solace in the freedom of being their own protectors, their own guardians, their own leaders. Their liberation was both personal and national.

Wallace was central to the idea of a free, independent

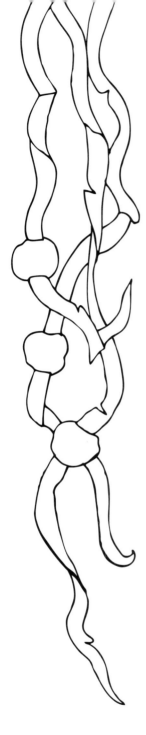

and self-made Scotland. But not even he could live out the war. Soon, to Scotland's horror, he was betrayed, captured and transported to London for trial. Grief shot through the nation as the news arrived that Scotland's highest guardian had been mockingly crowned by the English king before being publicly and gruesomely executed, and that parts of him were to be sent all over to insult and dishonour him.

'But tyranny is proverbially short-sighted,' announced the Rev. James Barr at a rally for Home Rule at Wallace's birthplace in 1921. 'It was the wrongs and indignities to which Wallace was subjected that rallied the Scottish people to the support of the national cause. When Edward crowned Wallace in mockery, although he knew nothing of it, he was putting a kingly and immortal crown upon his brow; and crowning him, not in London alone, but in the eyes of the world for all time. And when he transfixed his dismembered body on the gates of our northern burghs, he really laid all Scotland at the feet of Wallace, who welded the Scottish nation together for evermore.'

The martyrdom of Wallace both outraged and emboldened the Scots. Now there was absolute clarity that for Scotland to be distinct, for Scotland to have memory, for Scotland even to have a name, it had to fight for its independence. There was no half-way house, no middle option – 'Let us do or die!' as Robert Burns later wrote.

Wallace, during his trial for treason, captured the overwhelming sentiment of his country when he remarked that he couldn't be a traitor to Edward as he was never his subject. So words were the great orator's final weapon. The culture in which the Declaration of Arbroath would soon be written was one which shared that keen understanding of the power of words.

For too long now Scotland had been without a king. An underground movement of the Scottish church began to seek out a new leader who could emulate Wallace's passionate defence of the kingdom. A new King of Scots, Robert the Bruce, was soon propelled to the throne. Walter Bower announced the arrival of Bruce as a mercy from God to save the Scots from 'lying in a pool of misery and utterly lacking any hope of help or salvation.'

Robert the Bruce stepped up, and despite earlier flirtations with English allegiance he took the spirit of Wallace and de Moray to heart. In the eyes of the Scots he redeemed himself, he found his calling, the spirit of Scotland touched and changed him, he committed himself fully to the independence of Scotland and the community of the realm, and he vowed to carry the cause with purpose and sincerity. New followers united behind him, and the ranks of his ramshackle armies swelled.

All the while in England, Edward I, 'the Hammer of the Scots', *Malleus Scotorum*, deteriorated and died. His dying wish was to have his bones carried into further battles to conquer his troublesome northern neighbour. But the death of the tyrant gave little peace to the Scots, for soon Edward's son, Edward II, inherited his father's crown, as well as his hunger for

16

conquest, and vowed to eliminate Bruce and the Scots once and for all.

This new English king was young and resolute. He marched north with a superbly equipped army, aiming to utterly wipe out 'Robert de Brus who calls himself King of Scotland'. In 1314 the English army struck at the very heart of Scotland, the town of Stirling. They were so certain of victory they took a poet with them to record the battle in glorious verse. But when the English army arrived they were met on the outskirts of a small nearby village, and to their surprise were utterly routed by Bruce's men. The name of this otherwise insignificant village was soon ringing with disbelief through the courts of Europe: Bannockburn.

Edward II panicked and fled the scene with his bodyguard, his remaining foot soldiers left to flee 90 miles south to the English border. The Scots were triumphant but exhausted. They hoped their unexpected victory would give them diplomatic weight and legitimacy in Europe, and that it would allow them to assert once and for all their hard-won independence and refute English claims of overlordship.

Victory at Bannockburn bought the Scots time to drop the sword and pick up the pen. It was agreed a diplomatic letter should be sent to Pope John XXII in Avignon, the United Nations of the day, calling for him to recognise Scotland's independence and admonish the English king. The writing duty was given to the Scottish church, as holy men were literate and could evoke the right sentiments to engage the Pope's attention. An abbey was chosen on the east coast of

Scotland, safe from the threat of English invasion and facing Europe across the water. And so in 1320 we reach Arbroath, ink and parchment at the ready, and the central subject of our story, the writing of that famous Declaration.

THE ILLUSTRATED DECLARATION OF ARBROATH

The following pages contain a translation of the Declaration of Arbroath from the original Latin into English, used with permission from the National Records of Scotland. Full information on the source can be found in the acknowledgements at the end of this book.

Most Holy Father, we know and from the chronicles and books of the ancients we find that among other famous nations our own, the Scots, has been graced with widespread renown. It journeyed from Greater Scythia by way of the Tyrrhenian Sea and the Pillars of Hercules, and dwelt for a long course of time in Spain among the most savage peoples, but nowhere could it be subdued by any people, however barbarous. Thence it came, twelve hundred years after the people of Israel crossed the Red Sea, to its home in the west where it still lives today. The Britons it first drove out, the Picts it utterly destroyed, and, even though very often assailed by the Norwegians, the Danes and the English, it took possession of that home with many victories and untold efforts; and, as the histories of old time bear witness, they have held it free of all servitude ever since. In their kingdom there have reigned one hundred and thirteen kings of their own royal stock, the line unbroken by a single foreigner.

The high qualities and merits of these people, were they not otherwise manifest, shine forth clearly enough from this: that the King of kings and Lord of lords, our Lord Jesus Christ, after His Passion and Resurrection, called them, even though settled in the uttermost parts of the earth, almost the first to His most holy faith. Nor did He wish them to be confirmed in that faith by merely anyone but by the first of His Apostles - by calling, though second or third in rank - the most gentle Saint Andrew, the Blessed Peter's brother, and desired him to keep them under his protection as their patron for ever.

The Most Holy Fathers your predecessors gave careful heed to these things and strengthened this same kingdom and people with many favours and numerous privileges, as being the special charge of the Blessed Peter's brother. Thus our people under their protection did indeed live in freedom and peace up to the time when that mighty prince the King of the English, Edward, the father of the one who reigns today, when our kingdom had no head and our people harboured no malice or treachery and were then unused to wars or invasions, came in a guise of a friend and ally to harass them as an enemy. The deeds of cruelty, massacre, violence, pillage, arson, imprisoning prelates, burning down monasteries, robbing and killing monks and nuns and yet other outrages without number which he committed against our people, sparing neither age nor sex, religion nor rank, no-one could describe nor fully imagine unless he had seen them with his own eyes.

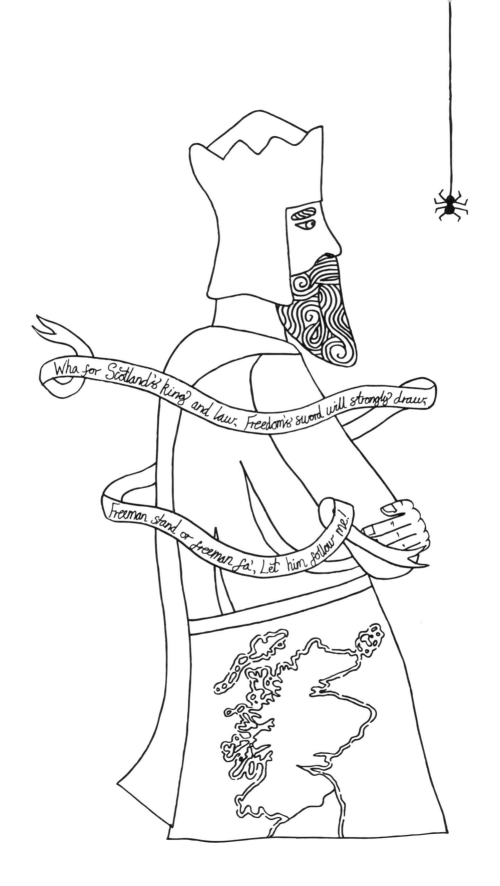

But from these countless evils we have been set free, by the help of Him who though He afflicts yet heals and restores, by our most tireless prince, King and lord, the lord Robert. He, that his people and his heritage might be delivered out of the hands of our enemies, bore cheerfully toil and fatigue, hunger and peril, like another Maccabaeus or Joshua. Him, too, divine providence, the succession to his right according to our laws and customs which we shall maintain to the death, and the due consent and assent of us all have made our prince and king. To him, as to the man by whom salvation has been wrought unto our people, we are bound both by his right and by his merits that our freedom may be still maintained, and by him, come what may, we mean to stand. Yet if he should give up what he has begun, seeking to make us or our kingdom subject to the King of England or the English, we should exert ourselves at once to drive him out as our enemy and a subverter of his own right and ours, and make some other man who was well able to defend us our King;

For, as long as a hundred of us remain al
to the lordship of the English. It is in tr
fight, but for freedom alone, which

er will we on any conditions be subjected
for glory, nor riches, nor honours that we
est man gives up but with life itself.

Therefore it is, Reverend Father and Lord, that we beseech your Holiness with our most earnest prayers and suppliant hearts, inasmuch as you will in your sincerity and goodness consider all this, that, since with Him Whose vice-gerent on earth you are there is neither weighing nor distinction of Jew and Greek, Scotsman or Englishman, you will look with the eyes of a father on the troubles and privations brought by the English upon us and upon the Church of God. May it please you to admonish and exhort the King of the English, who ought to be satisfied with what belongs to him since England used once to be enough for seven kings or more, to leave us Scots in peace, who live in this poor little Scotland, beyond which there is no dwelling-place at all, and covet nothing but our own. We are sincerely willing to do anything for him, having regard to our condition, that we can, to win peace for ourselves.

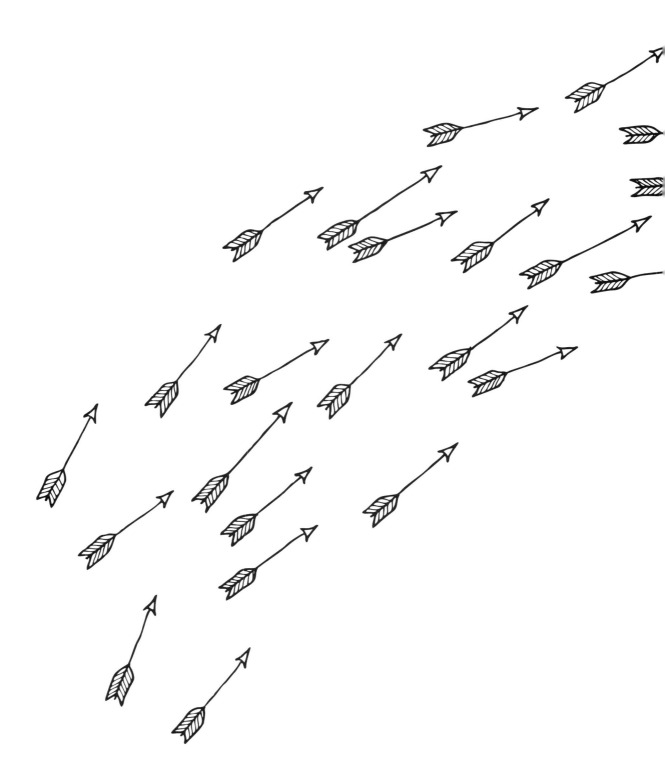

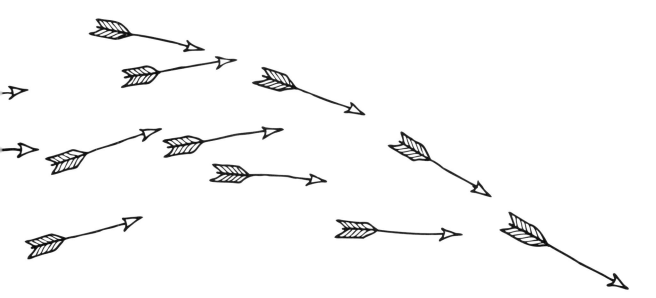

This truly concerns you, Holy Father, since you see the savagery of the heathen raging against the Christians, as the sins of Christians have indeed deserved, and the frontiers of Christendom being pressed inward every day; and how much it will tarnish your Holiness's memory if (which God forbid) the Church suffers eclipse or scandal in any branch of it during your time, you must perceive. Then rouse the Christian princes who for false reasons pretend that they cannot go to the help of the Holy Land because of wars they have on hand with their neighbours. The real reason that prevents them is that in making war on their smaller neighbours they find a readier advantage and weaker resistance. But how cheerfully our lord the King and we too would go there if the King of the English would leave us in peace, He from Whom nothing is hidden well knows; and we profess and declare it to you as the Vicar of Christ and to all Christendom.

But if your Holiness puts too much faith in the tales the English tell and will not give sincere belief to all this, nor refrain from favouring them to our undoing, then the slaughter of bodies, the perdition of souls, and all the other misfortunes that will follow, inflicted by them on us and by us on them, will, we believe, be surely laid by the Most High to your charge. To conclude, we are and shall ever be, as far as duty calls us, ready to do your will in all things, as obedient sons to you as His Vicar, and to Him as the Supreme King and Judge we commit the maintenance of our cause, casting our cares upon Him and firmly trusting that He will inspire us with courage and bring our enemies to nothing. May the Most High preserve you to His Holy Church in holiness and health for many days to come. Given at the monastery of Arbroath in Scotland on the sixth day of the month of April in the year of grace thirteen hundred and twenty and the fifteenth year of the reign of our King aforesaid.

POOR LITTLE SCOTLAND

There we have it, one of the most significant statements of nationhood and freedom ever made. After a list of signatories, this ancient manifesto began, 'Most Holy Father, we know and from the chronicles and books of the ancients we find that among other famous nations our own, the Scots, has been graced with widespread renown.' What is so striking about these opening words is the emphasis placed upon Scotland's historical legitimacy as a nation; a legitimacy derived from the mysterious and unnamed 'books of the ancients'. It was books, after all, which were under threat of theft or burning at the hands of English raiders. It was books, and the ancient stories they contained, which empowered Scotland to defend its nationhood.

By recounting a foundation myth of the Scottish nation, journeying 'from Greater Scythia by way of the Tyrrhenian Sea and the Pillars of Hercules', the Declaration of Arbroath deep-rooted Scotland's origins to the very murkiest edges of the known world.

Long before a war of swords and shields there was

a war of myths, stories and books: destroy a nation's story and destroy the nation, but tell a nation's story and the nation survived.

But telling a good story, as the Declaration's writers would have known, would not be enough to save the Scottish kingdom. Being addressed to Pope John XXII the Declaration would not only have to emphasise Scotland's distinct nationhood but its devotion to the church. An emphasis on the patron saint, St Andrew, bridged nationality and faith in a way which positioned Scotland, though 'at the furthest ends of the earth', at the very heart of medieval Christendom.

The letter confirmed the profound significance of St Andrew to the Scots. The X-shape on which the saint was crucified had been adopted as a symbol of Scottish nationhood since, in a miracle long ago, it appeared in the sky above a battlefield in East Lothian.

According to Blind Harry, William Wallace's battle prayer was to say, 'St Andrew mot us speed' meaning 'St Andrew give us victory'. Scottish soldiers at Bannockburn also bore the white cross of St Andrew on their tunics, and knelt in prayer before the battle to evoke the saint's protection.

St Andrew gave the Scots a sense of holy protection in times of hardship and cruelty. Adopting Christ's first-called disciple as their patron also affirmed Scotland's special place in Christendom, the implied warning being that a nation under St Andrew's protection finding itself burnt-out and eliminated would be an affront to the Christian faith.

The backing of their church confirmed to the Scots

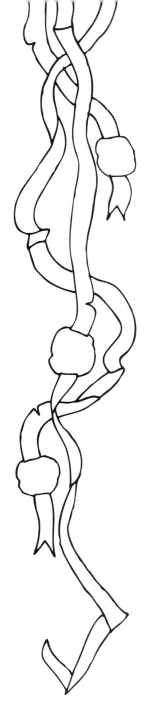

their cause was just, their resistance was legitimate and their nationality was due its place amongst the nations of God. To see the enemy burn down Scottish churches and monasteries only confirmed their belief that freedom was a holy cause.

Scottish holymen were vital to the campaign for independence. They emboldened the whole community of the realm to resist the English conquest. They were connected to the land and to the barons and had their own lines of communication to the churches of Europe. They publicly and veraciously supported the popular uprisings led by Wallace and de Moray. One Bishop of Glasgow, Robert Wishart, even fronted his own uprising in the west, leading to a spell in an English prison.

Nor did the Scottish church take issue in channelling its own funds into the resistance, which needed all the assistance available to it, financial, divine or otherwise. The Scottish church after all would not be spared from the total eradication of Scotland in Edward II's designs. If the English conquest was to be all-encompassing, church and all, so must be the response.

The evocation of holy powers gave authority and weight to Scotland's burgeoning community of the realm. Literate churchmen had the skill to articulate the hopes of an illiterate populace, providing Biblical examples of other peoples in other lands who had overcome terrible injustices and emancipated themselves from overbearing tyranny. One primary teaching of the Bible after all was the possibility of transformation; that everything could be different, that miracles could be performed, that prayers could be answered, that even the dead could be resurrected.

The rebirth of Christ after his crucifixion was an encouraging allegory to the idea that Scotland too, against all the odds, could be saved and reborn. It allowed Scots to imagine Wallace the martyr outliving his gruesome execution, and his spirit living on in the continuing fight for independence.

What made the Declaration's rhetoric so persuasive was the way it set out contrasts and oppositions; freedom versus subjection, peace versus warmongering, small nation versus brute strength. Scotland 'did indeed live in freedom and peace' and 'harboured no malice' towards its southern neighbour until the English conquest, it said.

Nor did the Declaration make any secret of the 'countless evils' of life under English rule, and the ruinous state in which the country had been left by the tyranny of both Edwards. It said 'The deeds of cruelty, massacre, violence, pillage, arson, imprisoning prelates, burning down monasteries, robbing and killing monks and nuns and yet other outrages without number which he committed against our people, sparing neither age nor sex, religion nor rank, no-one could describe nor fully imagine unless he had seen them with his own eyes.' Anyone receiving such news would be left to picture the burnt-out carcass of Scotland after it had been subjected to such inhumanity, and the determination of the Scots to see it all one day restored and remade.

Love of Scotland shone through every word of the Declaration, but its writers never overstated the strength of their kingdom. They remained rather humble about that 'poor little Scotland, beyond which there is no dwelling place at all.' Nor did the document call for revenge against the English; it asked only for Scotland to be a nation free amongst others, and to be left in peace to recover and rebuild.

Rebuilding was a task to be given to Scotland's emergent king, Robert the Bruce. The Declaration made no half-measures in its endorsement of him, comparing King Robert to Maccabaeus, the ancient leader of a Jewish revolt, or Joshua, who assisted Moses in leading the Israelites out of Egypt. The Declaration pledged in earnestness: 'To him, as to the man by whom salvation has been wrought unto our people, we are bound both by his right and by his merits that our freedom may be still maintained, and by him, come what may, we mean to stand.'

Of Robert the Bruce's role as king, it went on to say: 'Yet if he should give up what he has begun, seeking to make us or our kingdom subject to the King of England or the English, we should exert ourselves at once to drive him out as our enemy and a subverter of his own right and ours, and make some other man who was well able to defend us our King.' A king ruling only by the given consent of his people was no less than revolutionary in the Europe of 1320.

Robert the Bruce, though his earlier life was one of hunger for power, eventually signed away his own privileges, his own right to rule, in the Declaration of

Arbroath. A promise was made: Bruce was king for as long as he did the job, and the good governance of the kingdom was of higher importance than the person who ruled it.

It's here the Declaration reached its most famous crescendo: 'For, as long as a hundred of us remain alive, never will we on any conditions be subjected to the lordship of the English.' And then, one of the most evocative and profound strikes for freedom in the written history of the world: 'It is in truth not for glory, nor riches, nor honours that we are fighting, but for freedom alone, which no honest man gives up but with life itself.'

The Declaration ended with what the Scots hoped would be an appealing offer to the papal authorities; bring an end to the English conquest and the Scots would be free to assist the Pope's crusades on the far edges of Europe. But that olive branch was quickly darkened by a stark warning against the Pope's reputation should he ignore the Scottish plea: 'But if your Holiness puts too much faith in the tales the English tell and will not give sincere belief to all this, nor refrain from favouring them to our undoing, then the slaughter of bodies, the perdition of souls, and all the other misfortunes that will follow, inflicted by them on us and by us on them, will, we believe, be surely laid by the Most High to your charge.'

When Scottish ambassadors arrived in the heat of the Avignon summer in 1320, they couldn't have known what kind of response their precious letter would receive. Pope John XXII, encased within the

high walls of his white palace, was known as a man of law and order. He wasn't the most obvious sympathiser to Scottish ideas of legitimate resistance and deposing their own king if they had to.

But the response from the papal court in Avignon was tentatively encouraging. Pope John himself wrote to the English king, quoting from the Declaration of Arbroath, telling him to halt the invasion and make peace with his northern neighbour. Robert the Bruce was even referred to as 'Robert Illustrious king of Scotland', a far cry from the previous 'Robert Bruce governing in Scotland'. After years of bloody war it appeared the security and recognition of an independent Scottish kingdom was finally achieved, in no insignificant part, by good peaceful diplomacy and the transformative power of words.

Nationalism around the world has sometimes been associated with a desire to overstate the power and greatness of a nation. But written into the Declaration of Arbroath was an altogether different kind of nationalism: one which was humble, one which admitted weakness, one which recognised smallness and vulnerability and one which reached out for international friendship and co-operation. It perfectly illustrated the simplicity and humanity of Scotland's demands for independence in contrast to the bravado of the English conquest. England itself, the Declaration pointed out, was once 'enough for seven kings or more'.

The common humanity at the heart of the Declaration made it easily comprehensible across national boundaries. The Scots were determined to survive, and to survive as Scots, with or without the blessing of the Pope. But his favourable judgement would come as a great relief to those eagerly awaiting a response at home.

At a time when most of Europe was still powered by loyalty to absolute monarchs, it was the Scots, in their Declaration, who made ground-breaking advances towards new ideas of nationhood. It was the Scots who first articulated a now commonly held belief: that the collective endeavour of a people could take precedence over traditional structures of authority and centralised power. After 1320, what it meant to be a member of a community, what it meant to be a citizen of a country, was forever redefined.

TREE OF LIBERTY

In time war with England came to an end, and the relative peace of a free and independent Scotland was secured for several hundred years. But stories of the struggle were not quickly forgotten. A vision of a hard-won freedom was implanted firmly in the Scottish memory. Stories of Bruce and Wallace, and the noble sentiments of the Declaration of Arbroath, were reimagined in poems, books and letters long after the event.

One of the first books ever printed in Scotland was *The Wallace* by Blind Harry, a romantic epic following the life of William Wallace in his noble quest for Scottish freedom. For several centuries *The Wallace* and The Bible were the two books most commonly found in Scottish homes.

Retellings of the lives of Wallace and Bruce and their roles in the Wars of Independence were undyingly popular. But the Declaration of Arbroath itself, for one reason or another, was never reprinted in text with equivalent enthusiasm. Perhaps it lacked the everyman

adventure of Wallace or the chivalric romance of Bruce. Perhaps, amidst the Protestant Reformation of the 16th century, when Scotland's ties to the Catholic church were cut, a devout letter to the Pope simply fell out of fashion.

All that being said, the Declaration was not unknown to the Covenanters, Scottish Protestants of the 17th century who fought to preserve Scotland's religious independence against King Charles I's attempts to introduce an Anglified style of worship.

It could even be said the Covenanters were responsible for writing the most significant declaration in Scotland since 1320. Their National Covenant, like a large petition, was distributed around churches encouraging supporters to put their names to the cause of preserving Scotland's religious freedoms.

In his book *Scottish Covenanters*, the Rev. James Barr described the Covenanting movement as 'the pioneers of full civil and religious freedom' who 'stood for the rule of the people against the domination of arbitrary princes.' He even went as far as to say 'The Covenanters were really resisting a movement, which has gone on to this hour, to eliminate the boundary between Scotland and England; to make Scotland but an outlying province of England … The Covenanters were asserting our Scottish Nationalism in the sphere of religion, and seeking to maintain our ancient Scottish independence.'

The Covenanters, in the eyes of this Presbyterian relative of mine, honoured and upheld the principles of the Declaration of Arbroath, only remoulded into another time and struggle. Such a view was enthusiastically shared by the writer John Galt, who published a novel on the Covenanters called *Ringan Gilhaize* with a full translation of the Declaration of Arbroath in the appendix. It hardly mattered that the Declaration was a Catholic document and the Covenanters were Protestants; both were part of a tradition of written resistance, and of a particular kind of Scottish liberty in which no injustice could go passively tolerated.

Only a few decades on from the height of the Covenanting movement, memories of the past re-surfaced again, this time amidst fiery debate over the 1707 Act of Union. A political treaty was drawn up to unite Scotland and England under one sovereign parliament in London, forming a United Kingdom of Great Britain and bringing an end to centuries of hard-won Scottish independence. Edinburgh printers frantically distributed anti-Union pamphlets referencing the ancient liberties secured in the Declaration of Arbroath, urging those freedoms to be upheld and for the treaty to be rejected.

Controversy was heightened further when an English lawyer claimed Union negotiations with the Scots were unnecessary because English kings had always claimed overlordship of Scotland. Infuriated, the Scottish Parliament had the lawyer's books ceremonially burned on the cobbles of Edinburgh. The Scottish Parliament also paid a high sum for its own historian to republish the kingdom's ancient constitutional documents, reasserting its long standing as a free and independent

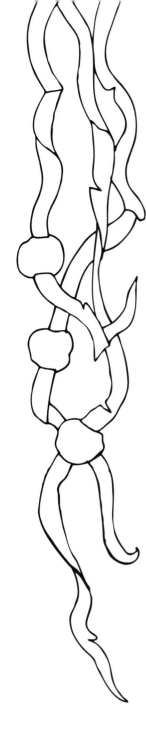

country. The Anglo-Scottish war of books, for a moment, had returned.

To Andrew Fletcher of Saltoun, an East Lothian laird and parliamentarian raised firmly in the traditions of the Declaration, the Union was something to be firmly resisted. For Fletcher, large and expanding nation-states made government remote and unaccountable, and fostered corruption and injustice, whereas smaller independent states preserved individual liberties and were better able to advance the well-being of their citizens.

Fletcher was concerned chiefly with justice and injustice: justice between people, justice between nations, justice between the governing and the governed. He believed, in line with the traditions of the Declaration, that government derived its authority from the consent of the community. And, in line with the Declaration's clause on kingship, he believed any ruler who proved themselves unfit to govern forfeited their right to the crown.

But Fletcher's moral integrity was not wholly matched by his fellow countrymen. The Scottish Parliament's initial distaste for the Union weakened as corruption spread behind closed doors. Robert Burns, writing long after the event, criticised Scotland's parliamentarians who accepted the Union, calling them 'A Parcel of Rogues' for accepting substantial bribes from the English Government.

When the Act of Union took effect on 1 May 1707, amidst a deep haar, the bells of Edinburgh's St Giles' Cathedral rang to the tune 'Why should I be so sad on my wedding day?' capturing the sorrowful mood of the population. On the same day a pod of whales took a wrong turning in the Firth of Forth and beached themselves on the coast of Kirkcaldy. The number of whales matched the number of parliamentarians who approved the treaty, and their death was taken as an ill-omen for the marriage between the two nations.

The Union was passed, in the words of the Rev. James Barr, 'by the most shameless bribery ever known in the most corrupt ages of human history.' But no bribe, however large, could have ever moved the position of Fletcher of Saltoun. For Fletcher, those sentiments from the Declaration of Arbroath still rang true: not for riches, nor honours, nor glory, but for freedom, for that alone.

In years to come the new political arrangement with England won support amongst those who believed Scottish trade had benefitted from a broadened market, but for Fletcher the Union never achieved what might be called moral legitimacy. No number of merchants getting rich from the scheme could compensate for the loss of Scotland's ancient freedoms or the undignified way it all came about.

In hopelessness and despair, Fletcher turned his attention to farming, his oratory talents vanishing from the public forum. With his dying words in 1716 he delivered one final condemnation of Scotland's condition, uttering only 'Lord have mercy on my poor country which is so barbarously oppressed.'

Over the following half-century dissatisfaction with the Union continued to be manifest in the cause of

the Jacobites who, in line with the 1320 Declaration, asserted their right to choose a replacement king who was fit to defend their freedoms. From this turbulent century of competing ideas also came the poet Robert Burns, as political and radical a poet as ever there was, whose ideas of freedom were as much inspired by revolutions in Europe as they were by stories of Scotland's ancient past.

In 1793 Burns wrote 'Scots Wha Hae', a patriotic anthem recounting Robert the Bruce's march to the Battle of Bannockburn. But in a letter Burns admitted the song also disguised 'other struggles of the same nature, not quite so ancient,' referring to the plight of the political reformers of his own era.

In 1820, five centuries on from the Declaration of Arbroath, a Scottish Insurrection saw a week of strikes and unrest, with workers rallying to a banner emblazoned with the words, 'Scotland free or a desert!'

Memories of Scotland's long-distant fight for freedom even inspired the struggles of the Scottish Suffragettes. One report told that a suffragette invoked lines from 'Scots Wha Hae' and Bruce's freedom-fighting spirit as she refused to enter the dock. Another suffragette, Annie Knight, whose remarkable life spanned three centuries, was a champion of both women's rights and Scottish independence and became one of the founding members of the Scottish National Party.

Rarely through the centuries was the Declaration of Arbroath held up at the forefront of social change; whole movements could pass with it only being mentioned one or twice. But its message was still often there, faintly in the memory, a ghostly presence from the depths of history, a bedrock of Scottish political thought, an eternal affirmation of right over wrong, justice over injustice, underdog over tyrant.

And what of Arbroath Abbey itself? Throughout all of these changes the abbey crumbled away, practically unnoticed. Almost as soon as the Wars of Independence were over it began to disintegrate as if, having served its noble purpose, it could retire to ruin. Two English raids set the abbey to flame, then, once it had recovered, it was struck again by lightning and a fire went blazing through the fabric of the church.

By the time of the Protestant Reformation the building was thoroughly neglected, its red stones carted off into the adjacent town as building materials for houses. By the Act of Union the ruined carcass of the abbey matched the sombre and dilapidated mood of the nation. Its great towers collapsed and it was left, more or less, as it has remained to this day.

Sitting in the grounds of Arbroath Abbey, with the sun peering in through the great 'O', I remembered reading somewhere how the fortunes of ruined places began to change during the 19th century. The rising popularity of gothic novels, such as *Frankenstein* and *Dracula*, meant that many began to seek beauty in the decay and destruction of the ancient world.

The abbeys which once produced great works of medieval writing were now themselves, in part, saved by literature. New appreciation for ancient buildings meant, for the first time, measures were put in place to

preserve and restore them. But it wasn't until the early 20th century that the abbey returned to the political imagination, as an emerging Scottish nationalist movement began to value the red ruin as an icon of independence.

To these early nationalists, as few and as marginal as they might have been, Scottish history was something not only to be studied but to be revived and resurrected. By working in poetry, art and music, and by honing their talents for public debate, they would ensure the prevalent view of Scottish history, that all ideas of independence were long dead and buried, wouldn't last the coming century.

The Thistle Rises

For Scottish nationalists of the early 20th century, when a spirit of British unity was at its height, independence often seemed an impossibly far-off prospect. Even events which could have been cause for celebration or advancement, such as the 600th anniversary of the Declaration of Arbroath in 1920, were lost beneath a fog of tightly-managed officialdom, with all the political connotations of Scotland's ancient past remaining forgotten or overlooked.

The primary focus of the 1920 commemoration at Arbroath Abbey was a large party of magistrates, councillors, representatives of church and state, and other distinguished guests headed by the Provost of Arbroath.

With the exception perhaps of the Scottish Home Rule Association, the majority of those on the platform would not have been particularly interested in political nationalism. The first formation of a Scottish nationalist party, the National Party of Scotland, was still eight years down the line. This was a Scotland in

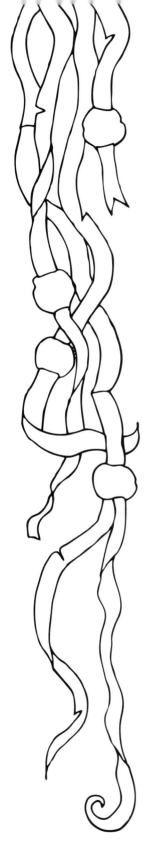

which the Union was very much secure, and in which terrible experiences in the recent war had meant an image of collective British sacrifice was fixed firmly in the Scottish imagination. The freedoms they came to celebrate at the 600th anniversary were more reminiscent of the freedoms won in the Great War than anything to do with a contemporary desire for Scottish independence.

The opening sentiments of the address given by the Moderator of the Church of Scotland were decidedly pro-Union. He expressed gratitude that Scotland had won its independence long ago, but only because it allowed Scotland to maintain its 'strong, robust character' which it now contributed so effectively towards the British Empire.

Little did these sentiments change as, one after the other, a line of officials made impassioned speeches on the glories of Scotland's ancient freedom struggle, only then to find all kinds of convoluted ways to explain why independence was no longer possible nor desirable.

One dissenting address was given by the Moderator of the United Free Church of Scotland, who related the Declaration of Arbroath's message to nations around the world which, at that time, were struggling against the Empire for their freedoms. The lesson from Scottish history, he said, was that it was not only wrong but impossible to govern a people against its will, and that self-determination was a human and natural right applicable to all nations. This was met by loud applause in the abbey. The mixed messages of the ceremony were ended with a rendition of 'Scots Wha

Hae' followed seamlessly by 'God Save the King'.

Later in the year, in October 1920, an early pro-independence organisation known as the Scots National League held an alternative gathering at Arbroath, free from the constraints set by men of church and state. It was supposed be led by the aristocratic Scottish nationalist Ruaraidh Erskine of Marr, who due to an illness had to step down. Marr was replaced by the famous socialist republican John Maclean, who drew a considerably larger crowd.

It was not long after that gathering my great-great-grandfather, the Rev. James Barr, came onto the scene as a leading advocate for Scottish self-government. A minister of the United Free Church, he was also a radical, a socialist, a pacifist, and a vocal advocate for teaching Scottish subjects in schools.

On being elected as an Independent Labour Party MP for Motherwell in 1924, the Rev. James Barr quickly set about laying the groundwork for Home Rule. But when he introduced his bill to the House of Commons both Labour and Conservatives proved uninterested, and the motion was unceremoniously dropped.

A change of mood swept the small but vocal national movement in Scotland. An emergency meeting was called in Glasgow, desperately seeking a way ahead, and the National Party of Scotland, later to become the Scottish National Party, was established in the following year.

What many nationalists wanted now was not a gradual advance but a critical moment, a burst of rejuvenation, a bolt of lightning in the national consciousness. In

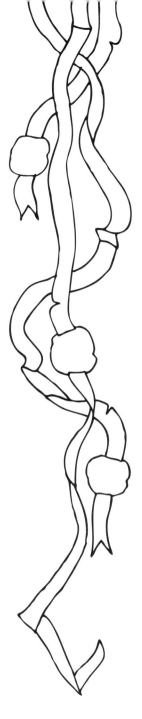

time that moment would come, and it would come, to the surprise of many, with the breathing of new life into an artefact of Scotland's ancient past – and one far older than the Declaration of Arbroath.

I remember when I was a student, first becoming aware of that other defining artefact of Scottish nationality, the Stone of Destiny, the ancient crowning stone of Scottish kings. The Stone was taken by an English army during the Wars of Independence and installed in Westminster Abbey where it sat for 700 years under the English throne. It remained there until Christmas Day 1950, when four students from the University of Glasgow drove down to London, broke into the abbey, lifted the Stone into the boot of their car and sped away with it into the night.

It was an unexpected moment of rebellion at a time when Scotland was otherwise politically dormant. A major police operation ensued, and the Anglo-Scottish border was shut for the first time in hundreds of years.

The Stone of Destiny only re-emerged, months later, when the students decided to deposit it within the ruins of Arbroath Abbey. It was a symbolic gesture; giving up the Stone to the authorities, but doing so in a place associated with an ancient plea for Scottish independence.

The leader of the heist, Ian Hamilton, wrote an account of the episode in his book *Stone of Destiny*. Reading it as a student, the juxtaposition between the young activists and the old stone intrigued and excited me. It imbued in me a sense that each generation could attach fresh meaning to even our most ancient stories and traditions. It fascinated me, too, to think something as plain as an undecorated stone could be attributed with so many aspirations for the future of the nation.

In the autumn of 2018 I visited Ian Hamilton at his home on the west coast of Scotland. He was then 93 years old and I was 26. When I arrived at the house, overlooking beautiful water and mountains, we sat down together in Ian's living room and he told me the Gaelic names of everything we could see in the landscape outside.

For years he had avoided any mention of the Stone, and was ashamed of the brashness of the account he wrote when he was young. But with the passing of time he began to view the whole episode with enormous pride.

'It was a great adventure,' he said.

I asked Ian about his decision to leave the Stone on the grass at Arbroath Abbey all those years ago, and whether it was solely due to its connection with the 1320 Declaration.

'Absolutely. Absolutely,' he said.

It was one final symbolic act, he explained, one last gesture to connect the ancient past with contemporary political desires. Ian recalled the moment they turned to walk away from the object they had risked everything for. They stood for a moment at the abbey gate, and looking down the nave they heard the words of 1320 speak: 'It is in truth not for glory, nor riches, nor honours that we are fighting, but for freedom alone, which no honest man gives up but with life itself.'

'I never saw the Stone again,' he said.

We then spoke in some detail about the upcoming 700th anniversary of the Declaration of Arbroath, and the fact that the words of the letter held meaning for so many despite hardly anyone ever having the chance to see the artefact in person. I suggested it was, like the Stone of Destiny, more important as a symbol than as a physical object, to which Ian replied, 'Ah yes, the power of icons. They seem to have power to evoke the past for people. In a way, it would be one way of defining a Scot. A Scot is someone who believes in the icons.'

The thought of national identity being linked in some way to recognising visual cues, such as stones or declarations or other artefacts interested me as an artist. It made me think how much I enjoyed using Scottish motifs in my drawings and how I still used them with their original meanings in mind: nationhood, endurance, independence.

Before I left, I asked Ian what his advice would be to today's young people who wanted to change the way things were, in Scotland or elsewhere, to which he replied, 'Oh, go ahead! If you don't, who will? It's your generation that matters, so for God's sake make it count!'

With that enthusiastic command I left Ian's home, and as I walked along the coast I thought about the 'power of icons', whether in stones or declarations, and the way in which people could become swept up in objects and ideas from a time many centuries before their own. I was fascinated by an idea that the meaning of ancient artefacts didn't always expire with time, nor were they necessarily confined to a single moment in history, but could reappear, repurposed and attributed to new causes and desires, in the never-ending turmoil and movement of a nation.

The Wrath of of Wendy Wood

Throughout world history nationalism has come in so many forms and varieties it has often been difficult to pin-point precisely what it is, except to say it is some way of imagining belonging to a nation. In some cases, nationalism has been exclusive and jingoistic, and in others inclusive and fluid. Nationalism, like all forces, is something which can be used for good or ill, but is not inherently one or the other. It is sometimes forgotten that different forms of nationalism have played vital roles in many of the world's progressive, emancipating and anti-colonial movements. Nationalism also inspired a great wealth of music, literature and art now celebrated far beyond its original borders.

Paradoxical as it may sound, nationalism done right has sometimes been best at reflecting our common humanity. This has been true in Scotland, thinking especially of Robert Burns, whose poetry was both patriotic and nationalistic, but also worldly, egalitarian and humanitarian; simultaneously 'Scots Wha Hae' and 'A Man's a Man'. Think too, of Hamish Henderson's

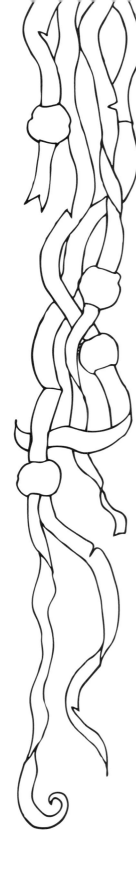

'Freedom Come All Ye', or of Winnie Ewing's famous election motto, 'Stop the world, Scotland wants to get on!'

Scottish nationalism has often been expressed not as a way of retreating from the world but a way of participating in it. In many respects this was true of the Declaration of Arbroath itself, a call for independence which deliberately linked Scotland to the canon of world history and appealed to universal human desires.

When I think of the kind of Scottish nationalism which was manifest in the early 20th century, and which took a renewed interest in the icons of independence such as the Declaration of Arbroath, I tend to think of people such as Wendy Wood, an English-born artist and campaigner for whom the cultural and political life of the nation were thought to be inseparable.

But Wendy Wood was also one of the early movement's most controversial figures. Her methods were unconventional, even extreme, spurning party politics to promote Scottish independence through a variety of direct actions, from removing Union Flags from public buildings to storming Stirling Castle. She spent several spells in prison, and even went on hunger strike in later life. When the Stone of Destiny went missing in 1950, though she played no part in the heist, it was assumed that only she could be responsible.

The poet Hugh MacDiarmid defended such an approach to Scottish nationalism at an Oxford Union debate in 1964, when he spoke on the same side as the American civil rights leader Malcolm X, supporting the motion that 'moderation in pursuit of justice is no virtue'. In his address, MacDiarmid recited the famous lines from the Declaration of Arbroath: 'For as long as a hundred of us remain alive, never will we on any conditions be subjected to English rule'.

'My people have done little but betray that oath ever since,' he said.

By the end of the 1960s Scottish nationalism, though still a marginal force, was well and truly on the rise. For most campaigners, pursuing change by more conventional means, the answer was to contest elections to the House of Commons, and in 1967 the SNP's first major breakthrough occurred when the young lawyer Winnie Ewing, against all the odds, won the Hamilton by-election.

Sensing the demand for self-government was on the rise, the Conservative Party took action, and several months later launched a 'Declaration of Perth', half-heartedly committing themselves to some form of Scottish devolution.

When the time came to mark the Declaration of Arbroath's 650th anniversary in April 1970, an interdenominational service at Arbroath Abbey went ahead as usual, but the provisions were low-key. The British Government, reluctant to give too much focus to the occasion, produced a single commemorative stamp. Not only that; it was decided the day's speeches would be headed by Willie Ross, the Secretary of State for Scotland, nicknamed 'Hammer of the Nats' for his intense dislike of Scottish nationalism.

Naturally the whole set-up was regarded as an insult by those who believed the Declaration of Arbroath

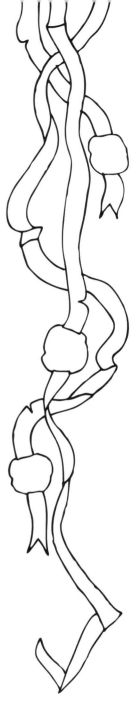

was an icon of Scottish independence.

In November 2018 I met Gordon Casely, who was a journalist at the time of the 650th anniversary. He talked me through the day's proceedings at Arbroath Abbey.

'It was a rainy day in April 1970' he said, 'I was 26 at the time, a young journalist, the same age as you are now. There's no doubt the audience was overwhelmingly unionist, as Scotland was back then. Entry to the event was by invitation only. Great churchmen, great judges, MPs, men of state and so on. That said, Wendy Wood was there too. She had been invited through the post. It was fascinating to see her there in amongst all those people.'

'Maybe inviting her was less trouble than not inviting her,' I suggested.

Gordon laughed. 'I think you may be right, Andrew!'

When Gordon told me what happened next it was clear his memory of the incident was still vivid: just as the Secretary of State for Scotland was about to address the abbey, Wendy Wood got to her feet and, in a clear ringing voice, pronounced the single word: 'Hypocrite!'

'The word reverberated round the walls of the abbey,' said Gordon with a smile, 'Everyone heard it. The security personnel were quite agitated.'

I imagined that word ringing round those ancient walls, sharp and accusing, just as Gordon described it, and the silent satisfaction of Wendy Wood as she returned to her seat. The brazenness of the act had obviously left a distinct impression.

'Wendy Wood was constantly interesting,' he

continued. 'Compton Mackenzie dedicated his book *On Moral Courage* to Wendy. She had colossal moral courage. Even most of her detractors couldn't help but admire her.'

Gordon reached into his bag and pulled out a vibrant blue pamphlet with a Saltire across the front. It was the official publication from the 650th commemoration, still wrinkled from the rain that fell over the abbey that morning all those years ago. I felt grateful when he gave it to me to keep.

Not long after, I came across a newspaper clipping from 1981, the year Wendy Wood died. She was due to appear at yet another commemorative pageant at Arbroath Abbey, but passed away not long before it. Her opening words were found in her papers and read aloud by a commentator in her stead. 'When you leave this holy place,' she would have said, 'may the spirits of Sir William Wallace and King Robert the Bruce be in you, to achieve the independence of Scotland ... Soara Alba!'

Sanctissimo Patri in Christo ac Domino, domino Johanni, divina providencia Sacrosancte Romane et Universalis Ecclesie Summo Pontifici, Filii Sui Humiles et devoti Duncanus Comes de Fyf, Thomas Ranulphi Comes Moravie Dominus Manie et Vallis Anandie, Patricius de Dunbar Comes Marchie, Malisius Comes de Stratherne, Malcolmus Comes de Levenax, Willelmus Comes de Roos, Magnus Comes Cathanie et Orkadie et Willelmus Comes Sutherlandie, Walterus Senescallus Scocie, Willelmus de Soules Buttonarius Scocie, Jacobus Dominus de Duglas, Rogerus de Mowbray, David de Graham, Ingeramus de Umfravile, Johannes de Meneteth Custos Comitatus de Menetethe, Alexander de Abernethy, Gilbertus de Haya Constabularius Scocie, Robertus de Keth Mariscallus Scocie, Henricus de Sancto claro, Johannes de Graham, David de Lindesay, Willelmus Olyfaunt, Patricius de Graham, Johannes de Fentoun, Willelmus de Abernithy, David de Wemys, Willelmus de Mountefichet, Fergusius de Ardrossan, Eustachius de Maxwell, Willelmus de Ramesay, Willelmus de Montealto, Alanus de Moravia, Douenaldus Cambrun, Reginaldus le chen, Alexander de Setoun, Andreas de Leslye, et Alexander de Stratoun, Ceterique Barones et liberetenentes ac tota Communitas Regni Scocie, omnimodam Reverenciam filialem cum deuotis Pedum osculis beatorum. Scimus, Sanctissime Pater et Domine, et ex antiquorum gestis et libris Colligimus quod inter ceteras nationes egregias nostra scilicet Scottorum nacio multis retro documentis insignita, de Magna Scithia per Mare tirenum et Columpnas Herculis transiens et in Hyspania inter ferocissimas gentes per multa temporum curricula residens, a nullis quantumcumque barbaricis poterat allicubi gentibus subiugari. Indeque veniens post undecim centum annos a transitu populi israelitici per mare rubrum sibi sedes in Occidente quas nunc optinet, expulsis primo Britonibus et Anglicos [sic?] sepius, multis cum victoriis et laboribus quamplurimis adquisivit, et Pictis omnino deletis, licet per Norwagienses, Danos et Anglicos sepius inpugnata fuerit, tenuit ab omni seruitute liberas Priscorum testatur Historia, semper tamen penitus indempnis. In quorum Regno Centum et Tredezim Reges de ipsorum Regali prosapia, nullo alienigena interveniente e Regnauerunt. Quorum Nobilitates et Merita, licet ex aliis non clarerent, satis patenter effulgerent ex eo quod Rex Regum et dominacium dominus Jhesus Christus post passionem suam Quam fidem Sanctissimam eos, velud in ulteriori terre fine positos, quasi primos ad suam fidem Sanctissiman convocauit. Nec eos per quemlibet in dicta fide confirmari voluit set per suum primum apostolum quamuis ordine secundum vel tercium sanctum Andream mitissimum beati Petri Germanum quem ipsos presse voluit et patronum. Hec autem Sanctissimi Patres et Predecessores vestri sollicita mente pensantes ipsum Regnum et populum ut beati Petri germani peculium multis fauoribus et priuilegiis quamplurimis Munierunt. Ita quippe quod gens nostra sub ipsorum proteccione hactenus libera degit et quieta donec Ille Princeps Magnificus Rex Anglorum Eduardus, pater istius qui nunc est, Regnum nostrum acephalum populumque nullius mali aut doli conscium nec bellis aut insultibus tunc assuetum sub amici et confederati specie, inimicabiliter infestauit. Cuius in iuiurias [...]

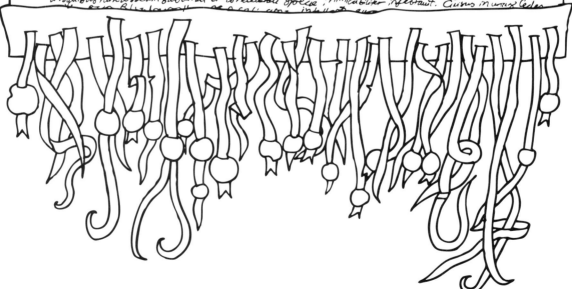

EPILOGUE

In the centuries of change and upheaval since the Declaration of Arbroath, the idea returned again and again that Scotland could be refashioned, remade and reborn.

The Scotland we inhabit today is a different country to the Scotland of 1320, and yet it is still the same land with the same name, the same borders, coast, mountains and rivers, and many of the same towns and settlements, albeit expanded, altered and rebuilt over time.

Traces of the Scotland of 1320 occasionally still loom over our skylines in ruined fortifications, churches and abbeys. Its symbols still appear in our flags and banners. Its languages are still spoken. Its most memorable events and characters are still living in the national imagination, and are still reanimated in books, plays and film. But most of all, and after all this time, questions of nationhood and sovereignty still carry weight in our politics.

In 2011, at the age of 19, I became involved in the

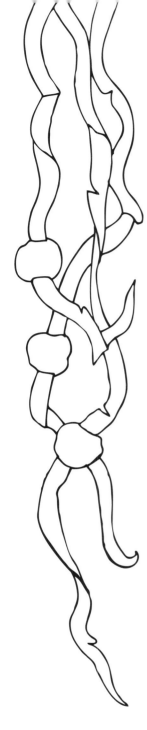

campaign preceding the 2014 Scottish independence referendum, an episode I detail in my first book *Summer of Independence: Stories from a Nation in the Making*. The campaign did not at first succeed, but the determination for Scotland's remaking would not go away. I realised from the old stories, such as that of the Declaration of Arbroath, that Scotland had always been transformed and remade, and always would be still.

The Declaration of Arbroath was largely absent from the 2014 referendum debate. The 'Yes' campaign had its eye fixed firmly on the future, and was pushing a vision of a modern, democratic and self-governing nation, a far cry from the Scotland of 1320. And yet the Declaration, even without being mentioned, still had presence in the vague and distant memory of the centuries as a kind of marker, a pertinent turning-point, when the Scots of long ago put pen to paper and declared themselves a nation, equal amongst all others.

The independence campaign never used the Declaration of Arbroath directly in its messaging, but it did devise its own 'Yes Declaration' with the aim of collecting one million signatures. Teams of campaigners took this new Declaration to the streets, and by August 2014 over one million Scots had signed. Perhaps for the first time since 1320, a document committing fully to Scottish independence had exercised the public imagination.

That summer, the independence movement was a flourishing festival of possibility, a cause of great hope and nobility, a creative, colourful affirmation of all that was best about people power, moral courage and self-belief. I believed then, as I do now, that a nation needed more to determine its future than arguments over oil, banking or currency. A nation, if it is to be transformed, needs the unashamed grandness of big dreams, free from pettiness and scepticism for scepticism's sake.

To me the Declaration of Arbroath is the embodiment of a Scotland which is humble and sincere, but also a Scotland with enormous capacity for dreams and visions, and a Scotland in which a sense of ourselves, however strong, is matched by an open hand of friendship to others.

In the centuries since the Declaration was written, Scotland has not always been generous in the way it has celebrated its own history. When independence was lost to the Union, self-doubt set in like a rot. A line from Shakespeare's *Macbeth* began to ring true: 'Stands Scotland where it did? … Alas, poor country, almost afraid to know itself.'

But hope of restoring self-consciousness to Scotland persisted, and over a long period of work by the nation's artists, writers and activists, the country was left in a much healthier place, better able to think of itself as an equal amongst the other nations of the world.

Nearing the end of this project I stood, in the midst of the abbey at Arbroath, contemplating not only the red ruin but everything which unfolded in that place long ago, and all it meant for the survival of a nation once faced with annihilation. When the Scots put pen to paper in 1320 they articulated the sadness and desperation of their country's plight, but also their

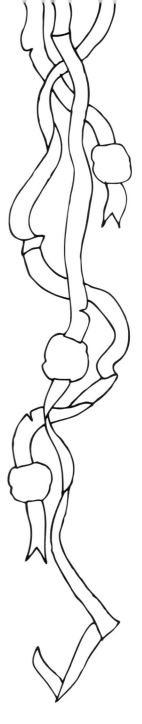

bright hope for its deliverance and transformation. That, to me, was always the magic and meaning of the Declaration, that a nation could be transformed, and could be transformed using the power of words.

Leaving the abbey, I considered how global history was full of people who overcame overwhelming odds to win all kinds of freedoms, and how the history of Scotland, and the Declaration of Arbroath contained within it, was just one fragment of that broader human story.

In its 700th anniversary year, and in all the years to come, let the Declaration of Arbroath be a reminder of Scotland's rightful place in the world as a nation equal amongst all others. Let it be a reminder of the power of community, and the importance of facing down tyranny and injustice. And let it be a reminder that, even when prospects look bleak and the odds seem overwhelming, there will always be a way for everything to be remade and transformed.

ACKNOWLEDGEMENTS

I would like to thank all those who offered advice and encouragement on the early drafts of the book, namely Alan Riach, Duncan Sneddon and James Robertson. I would also like to thank my sister Laura, who helped with the cover design, and the brilliant team at the Saltire Society, without whom this book might have never been made. Thanks are also due to the *Scots Independent* newspaper, which has been generous in supporting this project.

A number of books were useful in my research, namely *'For Freedom Alone'* by Edward J. Cowan (Birlinn, 2008); *The Declaration of Arbroath: History, Significance, Setting* edited by Geoffrey Barrow (Society of Antiquaries of Scotland, 2003); *A History Book for Scots* by Walter Bower and edited by D E R Watt (Mercat Press, 1998); *The Saltoun Papers: Reflections on Andrew Fletcher* edited by Paul Henderson Scott (Saltire Society, 2003); *On the Declaration of Arbroath* by Agnes Mure Mackenzie (Saltire Society, 1951);*The Scottish Covenanters* by Rev. James Barr (John Smith & Son, 1947); *Stone of*

Destiny by Ian Hamilton (Birlinn, 2008); *Yours Sincerely for Scotland* by Wendy Wood (Arthur Barker, 1970).

The translation of the Declaration of Arbroath used in this book was the revised 2005 version compiled by Alan Borthwick, based on *The Declaration of Arbroath, 1320* by Sir James Fergusson (Edinburgh University Press, 1970), with reference to *The Nation of Scots and the Declaration of Arbroath* by A A M Duncan (Historical Association, 1970), and *Scotichronicon* Vol. 7 edited by D E R Watt (Aberdeen University Press, 1996). The Declaration is Crown copyright, used with permission from the National Records of Scotland.

Last but not least, I would like to thank the following people, who were generous in their contributions to a crowd-funder for this book:

Terence Chan	Kate Doherty
David Morgan	Jennifer Owens
Ashley Douglas	Elspeth King
Ian Grant	Iain Wisely
Crawford Morris	Chris Clarkson
Elaine Fraser	James Lynch
Ian Hamilton	Lesley Backhouse
James Reid-Baxter	Kirk Torrance
Euan Campbell	Douglas Campbell
Allison Strachan	Laura Barr
David Barr	Lisl Richard
Mandy Farmer	Steve Byrne

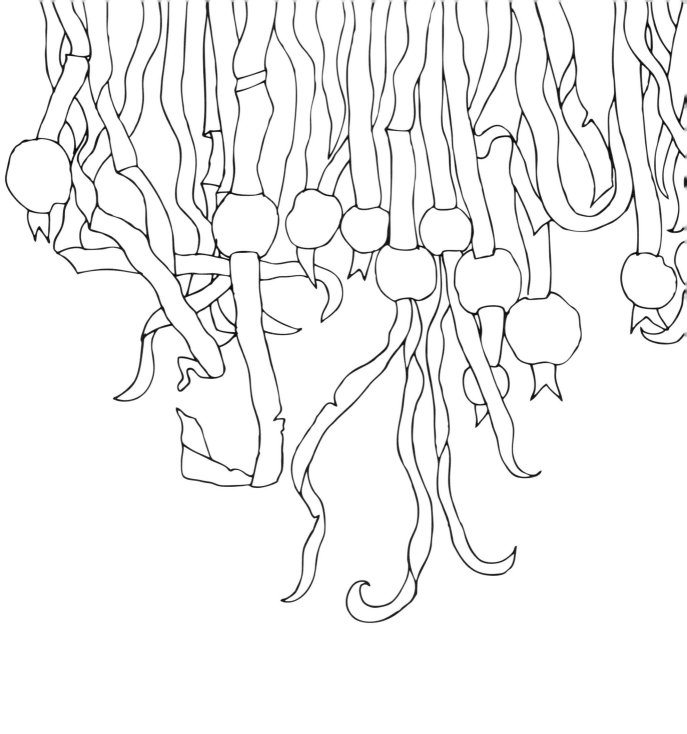